The Queen's Jewellery

The Queen's Jewellery

THE JEWELS OF H.M. QUEEN ELIZABETH II

SHEILA YOUNG

TAPLINGER PUBLISHING COMPANY
NEW YORK

First Published in the United States in 1969 by
TAPLINGER PUBLISHING CO., INC.
29 East Tenth Street
New York, New York 10003

SBN 8008–6565–0

Library of Congress Catalog Card Number 71–86660

Made and printed in Great Britain

Acknowledgements

Photographs reproduced by courtesy of: Asscher's Diamant; Baron Studios; Barratt's Photo Press; Camera Press; Central Press; Controller of Her Majesty's Stationery Office; Dorothy Laird; Fox Photos; Hay Wrightson; Keystone Press; Newcastle Chronicle and Journal; Paul Popper; Philip Antrobus; Press Association; Radio Times Hulton Picture Library; Sport and General; Topix; United Press.

I am most grateful to Buckingham Palace Press Office and Messrs. Garrard & Co. Ltd., The Crown Jewellers, for the considerable help they gave me in checking the facts in this book. S.Y.

List of colour plates

Her Majesty's Jewellery

To be a Queen Regnant must be, for any woman sensitive to the pulse of history, an altogether transcendent experience, rarely though the moments of realisation may come amid the din of modern living. In the reign of the first Elizabeth, the Queen's most passionate dramatist – the first great poet to write in modern English – made a King speak of

> . . . . the ripest fruit of all,
> That perfect bliss and sole felicity,
> The sweet fruition of an earthly crown.

An earthly crown is bedecked with jewels which can touch the neck of a queen centuries later. Jewels have an immortality which strangely links the most incongruous sovereigns, the bloody conqueror and the mild constitutional ruler. The King into whose mouth Christopher Marlowe put those dreaming words was called Tamburlaine, sometimes Amir Timur. Historically, he reigned 600 years ago, and massacred his way to the conquest of Persia, Afghanistan and India. A ruby which he indubitably owned, and presumably displayed in his turban-crown, is now part of a diamond-and-ruby necklace owned by Her Majesty Queen Elizabeth II of Great Britain. It is called the Timur Ruby and, weighing $352\frac{1}{2}$ carats, is the largest ruby known apart from the stone surmounting the Russian Imperial Crown.

Tartar tyrant and Tsar have passed; but Majesty remains, and needs its panoply. Marlowe made Tamburlaine turn to a brother monarch and call

> Is it not brave to be a King, Techelles?
> Is it not passing brave to be a King
> And ride in triumph through Persepolis?

The processions in triumph may occur more seldom today; the crackle of State papers and the cramp of administrative signature may whirl towards the vertigo of exhaustion: but the 'bravery' of monarchy must still be seen to be there – the moments of splendour must be observed and honoured. Even if it were not a normal counterpart of the balance of human nature and of the inherent gaiety of family life which in this case is lived in suites which are also parts of palaces, it would be the *duty* of the Queen occasionally to be clearly regal: but this natural woman smilingly bows to this duty

The constitutional historian Walter Bagehot, put the unanswerable case for splendour at Court. He said: 'There are arguments for not having a Court, and there are arguments for having a splendid Court; but there are no arguments for having a mean Court.'

Splendour at Court, on those occasions when it is deliberately sought, is expressed by ceremony, by ambience and dress which, though it should never be theatrical, is often breathtakingly 'out of this world' – and by the most cultivated revelation of most exquisite jewellery.

The ceremony is unsurpassed. The Court of Queen Elizabeth II has achieved the tone of dignity unsoiled by subservience which is the envy of citizens living under the protocol of many a republic. The ambience is inescapable. Whether in Buckingham Palace, Windsor Castle, or Holyroodhouse, no Sovereign could receive or entertain under conditions of graver majesty, richer tradition or more evocative art. The conservative magnificence of Court dress on a State occasion or at a formal banquet is legendary; it is balanced by a far greater number of occasions, launching a ship, quietly attending a theatre, or making a personal appearance to ten million television viewers, when sheer grandeur yields to a tasteful relationship with the normal wear of 'ordinary' people.

Apart from the qualities of her presence, her upbringing and the support of her family, the Queen's jewellery alone is enough to render her 'regal' in every circumstance.

The Queen's jewellery – which is distinct from the Crown Jewels is unique.

1   The diamond collet necklace and ear-rings worn here by the Queen were originally made for Queen Victoria from twenty-eight brilliant collets taken from a Garter Badge and from a ceremonial sword. The additional large drop-shaped diamond came from the Timur Ruby Necklace.

It is unique in value, which is perhaps the least of its qualities. The cost of replacement of the Queen's jewellery is incalculable. Her possessions are literally priceless.

It is unique in the field of craftsmanship linked with the history upon which it draws. There are pearls which were worn by Mary Queen of Scots and were sold to Queen Elizabeth I by her Regent when she lay in a Scottish jail, and worn by Gloriana in what was the great age of pearls as ascendant jewels. There are diamonds which have lain for centuries in the treasuries of Indian princes, some perhaps crudely cut by Antwerp standards but as interesting and 'untouchable' by modern renovators as, say, the Round Table of King Arthur in the hall of Winchester Castle. (Or who would re-cut now the rosecut Saint Edward's Sapphire, worn by our Saxon King Edward the Confessor in a ring 900 years ago, removed from his body as a holy relic, and now placed in the cross surmounting the Imperial State Crown?) There are ancient stones which have been re-designed, such as the thousand-year-old Koh-i-noor diamond – a Crown Jewel, incidentally, which Queen Elizabeth II has never worn and is never likely to, though Queen Victoria often used it as a brooch: it is now set (but removable) in the crown worn by the Queen Consort at the Coronations of King Edward VII, King George V and King George VI. It was originally abstracted from the Lahore Jewel Chamber of Ranjit Singh the Lion of the Punjab and was somewhat ineffectively cut under the supervision of the Prince Consort in 1862. A re-cut personal jewel of the Queen's, which she wore at her Coronation and many times since, is in the diamond collet necklace (Plate 1) originally made for Queen Victoria from 28 brilliant collets taken from a Garter Badge and from a ceremonial sword. To this was added the large drop-shaped diamond of over 22 carats which, in the photograph, the Queen is wearing suspended from the necklace proper. This magnificent stone came from the Timur Ruby Necklace, also once a part of the Treasury of Lahore, which was presented to Queen Victoria by the Honourable East India Company in 1851. But this diamond drop from the Timur Ruby Necklace (which held Tamburlaine's wonderful ruby) was trimmed, using the most modern approach and technique, as late as 1937, when it was reduced from 22·60 carats to 22·48 carats to be put

in the crown of Queen Elizabeth, now the Queen Mother, for the
Coronation of King George VI. (Plate 2). After this coronation the

2   For the Coronation in 1937 of Queen Elizabeth, now the Queen Mother,
the diamond drop from the Timur Ruby Necklace was trimmed for insertion
in the Queen's Crown. The stone is now worn (see Plate 1) by Queen Elizabeth II
as a pendant to Queen Victoria's diamond collet necklace which her mother is
wearing as a simple necklace in this picture.

diamond drop was put back on the necklace the Queen now wears.

Whatever are the triumphs of modern cutting – and perhaps the showpiece is the pair of diamond chandelier ear-rings (Plate 3) given to the Queen by her parents for her wedding, a set of jewellery which contains every known modern cut – the most brilliant period of sheer extrovert craftsmanship, particularly with diamonds, began in the late nineteenth century and originated in the magnificence of the Russian Imperial Court, then closely allied by blood ties with the British Throne. This was the time of the flowering of the tiara, as that ornament is at present known – the tiara has a curious history which will be recounted overleaf.

4   The Queen's first tiara, of diamond festoons, scrolls and collet-spikes, a wedding gift from Queen Mary and always a favourite with Her Majesty.

PHOTOGRAPH BY BARON
3   A masterpiece of modern cutting: the diamond chandelier ear-rings containing every known modern cut, a wedding present to the Queen from her parents.

5   Light and delicate, the Queen wears her first tiara to many functions, on the occasion illustrated at a Royal Festival Hall concert by the Hallé Orchestra.

Every lady of quality must look back with fond nostalgia to the time when she wore 'my first tiara', the great occasion it must have been, the people who were there . . . perhaps the one man. It is a perhaps surprising fact that until her marriage the Queen did not possess a tiara. Her first tiara was a wedding gift from Queen Mary, and it was the diamond tiara of festoons, scrolls and collet-spikes with 27 collets (Plate 4) which had been created in 1893 as a wedding present to Queen Mary herself from the Girls of Great Britain and Ireland. This is now a particular favourite of the Queen's, (see Plate 5) since it is very light in weight and delicate in appearance. Yet, for the ceremony of her wedding Princess Elizabeth, did not wear it. Following the tradition that she should wear 'something borrowed' she did in fact wear her mother's sunray fringed Russian-style tiara designed with vertical rows of diamonds graduating from a high point in the centre to a narrow band at the back (Plate 6). This

6   For her wedding the Queen wore 'something borrowed' . . . her mother's sunray fringed Russian-style tiara. Her double row of pearls were a wedding present from her parents.

BY KARSH OF OTTAWA

tiara, a possession of Queen Elizabeth the Queen Mother, is not the diamond fringe tiara (Plate 7) made in the Russian style which was originally presented by personal friends of Queen Alexandra in 1888 as a silver-wedding present. (Plate 8). This tiara was bequeathed to Queen Mary, who wore it on many occasions (Plate 9), and Queen

7, 8 & 9   In the portrait study by Karsh of Ottawa the Queen wears the diamond fringe tiara which was originally a wedding present to Queen Alexandra, who is seen wearing it in the picture top left. The tiara was inherited by Queen Mary, who often wore it *(top right),* and who subsequently bequeathed it to Her Majesty.

Elizabeth II subsequently inherited it from her grandmother.

Although it was the Court of the Tsar that had most influence in establishing the magnificence of present-day tiaras, this was a quite recent trend. The tiara was always kingly. The word originally connotated an ancient Persian turban, worn erect by the king and depressed, or crumpled, by others in the Court. Physically this progressed into the form of the Papal Tiara or triple crown, a high

10   Her Majesty wearing the triple row of pearls given to her in childhood by her grandfather King George V.

cap of gold cloth encircled by three coronets and surmounted by a gold cross, which was always the symbol of earthly sovereign power for the Pope, not a sacred symbol like the mitre. Modern tiaras trace back even farther to the diadem, the gold headband worn by ancient kings which has been found in the ruins of Troy and even in the tombs of the Chaldean kings who reigned 5000 years ago. The modern gem-set tiara, worn on the forepart of the head, often of a foliage or scroll design, was developed from the circlet-diadem worn by Empress Elizabeth of Russia and was initiated as a Court fashion set in France at the time of the first Napoleon. It became more elaborate amid the splendour of the Court of Saint Petersburg, and gifts of magnificent tiaras were made to members of the British Royal Family; they were worn on many State occasions abroad. However, during the closing years of the reign of Queen Victoria the Court in England was comparatively sombre and in Scotland non-existent. Only with the accession of King Edward VII and Queen Alexandra, did tiaras become almost a status symbol of nobility. Family jewels were withdrawn from the safe deposits of the mighty and re-set to intensify the unforgettable glitter of the Edwardian Court in its great resurgence of splendour.

Some magnificent tiaras were created. Her Majesty possesses eight of these beautiful pieces of jewellery now, but, as it has been noted, until her wedding she had none. Indeed, during girlhood, the Queen owned remarkably little jewellery. Her earliest treasure was a necklace, a triple row of pearls (Plate 10), given to her by her royal grandfather when she was very young – King George V died when Princess Elizabeth of York was only nine years old. She wore this necklace on many occasions in her childhood and through her teens, and continued to wear it when she had a far greater choice in her jewel case. This photograph was taken in 1963 when the Queen, making a tour of Australia, spoke to hundreds of listeners in the outback over the Flying Doctor service radio from the Flying Doctor base at Alice Springs.

There were two memorable gifts of jewellery from her parents while the Queen was still young. One was a diamond leaf shaped brooch with a centre of sapphires (Plate 11), and on another birthday occasion King George VI and Queen Elizabeth gave their daughter a pair of gold flower brooches with sapphire and diamond centres (Plate 12). Again it will be seen from the photographs that the Queen, now, often wears these mementoes of her father.

As her eighteenth birthday approached, the 21st of April 1944, she experienced an important change in her status which underlined her

11 *Above Left* A gift from her parents when she was a girl, frequently worn by the Queen now: a diamond leaf-shaped brooch with a centre of sapphires.

12 *Above right* Wearing this early birthday present from her parents brought the Queen luck at Kempton Park, where she saw one of her horses come in third. The jewellery is a pair of gold flower brooches with sapphire and diamond centres.

position as Heiress Presumptive. The King, who was regularly visiting his troops overseas and theatres of war like the blitzed island of Malta, asked that the Regency Act should be amended in order that Princess Elizabeth might be eligible to serve as a Counsellor of State at the age of eighteen instead of twenty-one, "in order that she should have every opportunity of gaining experience in the duties which would fall upon her in the event of her acceding to the Throne." The new Regency Act was passed, and Princess Elizabeth did serve as Counsellor of State almost immediately, when the King went to Italy. For this notable birthday – which was followed by the appointment of the Princess's first lady in waiting and the assumption of her first active public appointment (as President of the National Society for the Prevention of Cruelty to Children) – King George VI gave his daughter a sapphire and diamond bracelet of square sapphires and links of diamonds (Plate 13). Something of the loving care with which a Royal Family, with its treasury of jewels,

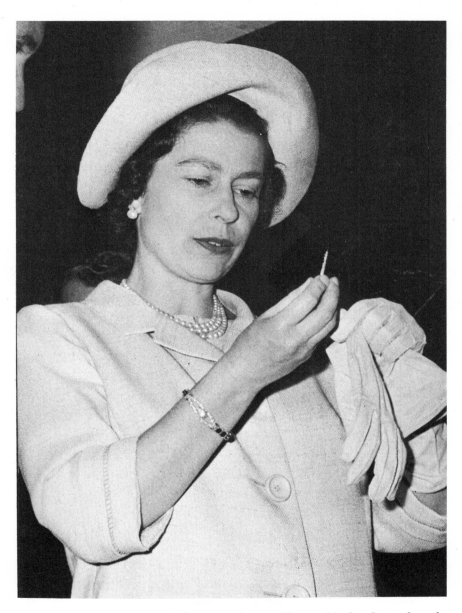

13   For her eighteenth birthday King George VI gave his daughter a bracelet
of square sapphires and links of diamonds . . . worn here by the Queen as she
examines a later present: a gold brooch replica of the Post Office Tower.

can plan for the future of a Queen may be guessed from the fact that on her wedding day (which was still three years distant) the King gave Princess Elizabeth a matching century-old necklace of oblong sapphires set in diamonds and sapphire drop ear-rings surrounded by diamonds (Plate 14).

14 An early Victorian necklace of oblong sapphires set in diamonds, with sapphire and diamond drop ear-rings, given as a wedding present to the Queen by her father. Her Majesty can be seen wearing it in Plate 25.

15   *Above left* The two aquamarine and diamond clips worn on the Queen's lapel can be joined into a brooch. They were an eighteenth birthday present to the Queen.

16   *Above right* An antique diamond flower brooch with a bow at the base of the stem, presented to the Queen by John Brown's yard when, as Princess Elizabeth, she launched H.M.S. *Vanguard.*

For her eighteenth birthday the Queen also received two aquamarine and diamond clips (Plate 15) which join into a brooch. In the same year she received as a present from John Brown's shipbuilding firm an antique diamond flower brooch with a little bow at the base of the stem (Plate 16) when she launched the battleship HMS *Vanguard* at Clydebank. This brooch came to have a special meaning for her, since it was in *Vanguard* that the Royal Family sailed for their South African tour in the spring of 1947 at a time which forced a particularly trying separation on Princess Elizabeth: for, though all hearts were willing, the formalities of State had not been completed, and her engagement to Prince Philip had not been announced. A launching memento, given a little later, became a particular favourite of the Queen. This was a flower brooch mounted in

26

17a & 17b   A platinum-mounted flower brooch with a raised centre of sapphires set in diamonds, presented to the Queen when she launched the oil-tanker *British Princess* at Sunderland, and worn here when the Queen opened the new Reading University.

platinum having a raised centre of sapphires with the petals set in diamonds (Plate 17a), the gift of Sir James Laing & Sons Limited and the Anglo-Iranian Oil Company Limited at the Sunderland launching by Princess Elizabeth in 1946 of the ship *British Princess*. She wore this (with the sapphire and diamond bracelet, Plate 13) at the christening of her daughter, Princess Anne, at Buckingham Palace on Trafalgar Day 1950 and also, as Queen, making her first Christmas Day broadcast from Sandringham in 1952.

Princess Elizabeth's twenty-first birthday coincided with her South African tour with her parents. She received as a birthday present from the Government and Union of South Africa what she unequivocally calls 'my best diamonds'. These were 21 large diamonds, cut and polished in Johannesburg and varying in size up to

18   "My best diamonds" is the Queen's description of the twenty-one diamonds given to her as a twenty-first birthday present from the Government of South Africa. The Queen is seen wearing them as they were first set, in a long necklace.

19 Later the twenty-one diamonds were divided, as is shown, to form a shorter necklace with a matching bracelet. The principal stone of the bracelet—the twenty-second stone in the set—was a gift from the De Beers Corporation.

ten carats. They were presented to the Princess to set as a necklace according to her own desires. There was absolutely no doubt that the Princess was overwhelmed at receiving them. They were presented in public in Capetown, and through a live microphone the vast audience as well as the listening public in the world outside heard the Princess's gasp of admiration and pleasure. At first these 21 diamonds were mounted to form a long necklace (Plate 18). Later it was decided to shorten the necklace, and early in 1952 this was done, and the remaining diamonds were mounted into a matching bracelet (Plate 19). One other exquisite diamond was needed to complete the bracelet and this was the gift of the De Beers Corporation.

20a All the children of Southern Rhodesia, black and white, gave the Queen as a twenty-first birthday present this diamond and platinum brooch depicting the flame lily.

20b   Princess Elizabeth wore the diamond and platinum brooch immediately the delegation of children presented it.

Another twenty-first birthday gift, of which the Queen is particularly fond, came from the pocket-money of all the children of Southern Rhodesia, black and white. It is a diamond and platinum brooch depicting the flame lily, the flower which was the emblem of Southern Rhodesia, and in order to make it a true replica a flower was

20c The twin ivy leaf brooches in diamonds were a twenty-first birthday present from King George VI and Queen Elizabeth.

plucked and flown to South Africa for an artist to sketch it for references before it faded. The Queen wore the brooch (Plate 20b) immediately she was presented with it, and she often wears it now when visiting children's homes, schools and hospitals. The Princess's gift from her parents was the twin ivy leaf brooches in diamonds (Plate 20c) which she wears now at the corner of a neckline, on her hat or on her lapel. From the Diplomatic Corps on this occasion she received ear-rings (Plate 21) each consisting of a diamond surrounded by eight diamonds.

Before Princess Elizabeth had left for South Africa she had 'launched' her first aircraft, naming a BOAC airliner *Elizabeth of England* and accepting the diamond brooch (Plate 22) which she has since worn when leaving London Airport on Commonwealth and North American tours. Soon after she returned home she was given the Freedom of the City of London: she was only the third woman to

21   The diamond ear-rings which the Queen is wearing in this picture (which also shows her tiara of festoons, scrolls and collet-spikes) was a twenty-first birthday present from the Diplomatic Corps.

26   Worn with her favourite light tiara, the Queen's necklace in this picture is the ruby and diamond necklace with a diamond drop pendant given to her by her parents as a wedding present.. The ruby and diamond ear-rings are Crown Jewellery.

22   The BOAC emblem as a diamond brooch was presented to the Queen when she named the BOAC airliner *Elizabeth of England*.

23   This diamond brooch depicting a lily was given to the Queen when she became only the third woman to receive the honour of the Freedom of the City of London.

27   When the Queen made her historic visit to the Vatican she wore the two strings of pearls with a diamond clasp. Her Majesty inherited them from her grandmother. With the pearls she wore Queen Alexandra's tiara.

receive this honour, her predecessor being Florence Nightingale. She was presented with the diamond lily-shaped brooch (Plate 23). But during the next months few public appearances were asked of her, though she accepted the Freedom of Edinburgh, for she was fully occupied in the elaborate planning of what for any woman, but so much more for the Heiress to a Throne, must be the most intricately organised day of her life.

On the 9th of July 1947 the engagement was announced between Princess Elizabeth and Lieutenant Philip Mountbatten, Royal Navy, subsequently created His Royal Highness the Prince Philip, Duke of Edinburgh, Earl of Merioneth and Baron Greenwich. The engagement ring, of which a unique jeweller's etching is shown (Plate 24), is a solitaire diamond supported by diamond shoulders, the stones being heirlooms belonging to Prince Philip's mother, Princess Andrew of Greece.

BY KIND PERMISSION OF PHILIP ANTROBUS LTD

24 A unique jeweller's etching of the Queen's engagement ring: a solitaire diamond with diamond shoulders, made from heirloom gems belonging to Prince Philip's mother.

And now it seemed that the treasure chests of the world were opening to the young Princess Elizabeth, and most particularly the private collection of the British Royal Family. There are three great crests in the momentum by which the Queen acquired the jewellery from which she can now choose, and this occasion, the first, is by far the happiest: not only because she was preparing to marry the man she loved and the world seemed to be rejoicing with her; but because also any further great acquisitions must necessarily be overshadowed by bereavement.

25 The magnificent sapphire and diamond suite of necklace with pendant, drop ear-rings and matching bracelet which the Queen has added after her original gift of the necklace and ear-rings (Plate 14) given to her by her parents for her wedding.

25a The sapphire and diamond tiara which the Queen is wearing was first seen in 1964.

It was now that King George VI brought out the necklace of oblong sapphires set in diamonds and separated by diamond collets, with the matching sapphire drop ear-rings surrounded by diamonds (Plate 25) on which his mind must have been dwelling since Princess Elizabeth's eighteenth birthday. This exquisite sapphire and diamond jewellery has been built up, through the Queen's married life, into what is perhaps her most imposing suite. In the summer of

1952 the necklace was shortened, and a pendant was added in the summer of 1959 (Plate 25). Soon afterwards a matching sapphire and diamond bracelet was added to the set. Towards the end of 1964 the Queen wore for the first time a new sapphire and diamond tiara (Plate 25a) which completes this elaborate suite. This jewellery might have been considered the principal wedding present of King George and Queen Elizabeth to their daughter had it not been for a 'rival' necklace which they also gave her: the ruby and diamond necklace with a diamond drop pendant which is splendidly shown in the colour plate (26). The ear-rings which are worn to match this necklace are Crown Jewellery, passing from sovereign to sovereign.

King George VI also gave Princess Elizabeth for her wedding a family heirloom, a double string of large pearls (Plate 6), which is actually two separate strings, one of 46 pearls which may have belonged to Queen Anne and the other of 50 pearls, which may have belonged to Queen Caroline, wife of George II. These can be worn as one, the clasps being a whole pearl. The string believed to belong to Queen Caroline was a fine necklace. She had four fine pearl necklaces, which she wore at the Coronation of George II. After the ceremony she had the most desirable pearls taken from the four and made into one superb necklace.

A further wedding present from the King and Queen to Princess Elizabeth was a long pair of diamond chandelier ear-rings with three drops which contains every modern cut. But it was four years before these beautiful jewels were worn (Plate 3). For, although Princess Elizabeth had begun to wear ear clips at the age of eighteen, she had not had her ears pierced. Just before she visited Canada in 1951 Princess Elizabeth had her ears pierced and later began to wear this magnificent present.

Breath-taking though the wedding presents from Princess Elizabeth's parents were, they were excelled by the gifts of Queen Mary, in whose personal possession lay many of the great pieces of late Victorian and of Edwardian jewellery. First Queen Mary gave her grand-daughter her tiara – 'Granny's tiara', it has been called by Her Majesty ever since. It is a tiara of diamond festoons scrolls and collet-spikes with 27 collets, and it was once Queen Mary's own wedding present, having been given to her on her marriage in 1893

28   Queen Mary wears the tiara of diamond festoons, scrolls and collet-spikes, a present given for her own wedding which she later gave to her eldest grand-daughter for her wedding to Prince Philip.

by subscription from the Girls of Great Britain and Ireland. It is interesting to see Queen Mary wearing it (Plate 28).

Queen Mary also gave Princess Elizabeth a diamond stomacher of intersected circles and half circles. The stomacher was re-intro-duced by Queen Alexandra after centuries of neglect, though it had

29 & 30   The diamond stomacher of intersected circles and half-circles given by Queen Mary on the occasion of Princess Elizabeth's marriage is seen complete at the right of the display of some of the wedding presents. The stomacher separates into three, and the Queen is seen wearing the smallest section as a brooch to hold the Garter ribbon.

31   This diamond bow brooch was another wedding
present from Queen Mary to Princess Elizabeth in
1947.

been a queenly ornament from the time of Elizabeth I to Louis XIV.
Queen Mary's original gift to her grand-daughter is eight inches
long, but Her Majesty uses the smallest part (Plate 29) – the stomacher
separates into three – which she often uses on State occasions to pin
to her shoulder the blue ribbon of the Garter.

Another wedding gift from Queen Mary was a brooch consisting
of a large diamond bow (Plate 31), originally presented to her by the
County of Dorset. Princess Elizabeth wore the brooch at the
christening of Prince Charles, now the Prince of Wales, and also
uses it to fasten her Garter ribbon. Not wishing to match the King
and Queen's gift of chandelier ear-rings, Queen Mary gave the
Princess a set of ear-rings for daytime use. (She had already given her
grand-daughter the pearl ear-rings (Plate 32) before the tour of
South Africa.) The bride now received the ear-rings consisting of one

32   For her first portrait with Prince Andrew the Queen wore the pearl earrings given to her by Queen Mary when she was twenty.

33 & 34   Ear-rings consisting of a large pearl suspended from a small
diamond were one of the Queen's wedding presents from Queen Mary,
who (opposite) can be seen wearing the jewels.

large pearl and a small diamond (Plate 33) which were originally
a wedding present to Queen Mary (Plate 34) from the County of
Devon, and additionally the diamond bracelets (Plates 35 & 36).
The first consists of two Indian diamond bracelets which the Queen
wears either separately or together. The second, diamonds with
rubies, was the County of Cornwall's wedding present to Queen
Mary.

BY KARSH OF OTTAWA

35 *(left)* Two Indian diamond bracelets which can be worn separately or together was one of Her Majesty's wedding presents from Queen Mary.

36 *(right)* The diamond and ruby bracelet which the Queen wears here was another wedding present from Queen Mary.

37, 38, 39 & 40 The bandeau tiara of English rose and foliage design worn by the Queen *(top left)*, was, with the diamond necklace worn by Her Majesty *(top right)*, a wedding present from the late Nizam of Hyderabad. The diamond rose centre clip on the tiara can be detached and worn *(bottom left)* as a brooch, and two smaller side roses can also be removed and worn *(bottom right)* as twin brooches.

41 The Queen wears the fringe diamond necklace in the Russian sunray design with the Diamond Diadem and part of Queen Mary's stomacher, worn as a brooch.

From outside the family came literally thousands of generous wedding gifts. Outstanding as jewellery is the bandeau tiara of English rose and foliage design (Plate 37) given by the late Nizam of Hyderabad with a matching necklace completed by a pendant (Plate 38). The diamond rose centre clip on the tiara is detachable, and can be used as a brooch (Plate 39), and there are two smaller side roses which can be detached (Plate 40) and are worn by the Queen on her lapel, at the corner of the neckline, and on her hat. The fringe diamond necklace threaded on silk (Plate 41) is of Russian design and was a wedding present to the Queen from the Lord Mayor and Aldermen of the City of London, The Governor of the Bank of England, the Chairman of the Stock Exchange, Lloyds and the Baltic Exchange and the Committee of the London Clearing Banks.

Perhaps the most poignant among the Queen's wedding presents, and certainly among the most valuable, is the Williamson pink diamond, now made up into the large flower brooch (Plates 42 & 43).

The donor, Dr John T. Williamson, was a solitary Canadian geologist burning with diamond fever who finally found his own mine in 1940 in what was then called Tanganyika. At the time the doctor was 33 years old. He ran his mine almost single-handed during the difficult days of the war and developed it into by far the richest-bearing diamond mine in the world. He stayed there, superintending guarded sorters who literally sorted the stones with one hand tied behind their back. In the solitude south of Lake Victoria, he died. But before he died he had made one shy gesture to the Crown.

His immense fortune affected him strangely. He bought a Rolls-Royce in Nairobi, but abandoned it in the dealer's showroom. He had overheard one malicious remark in a hotel bar. "So Williamson has bought a Rolls-Royce," said the gossip. "That's just what you would expect from a man who had never owned even a wheelbarrow in his life before."

He lived in the bush in a bungalow stacked with an overflow of Persian carpets, fine silver, first editions and antique furniture. He had a cellar of fine wines and old brandies, but he rarely drank anything but whisky and lime juice. His loneliness was soothed only

48

42 & 43   The 'Williamson pink', the world's finest rose-pink diamond, which is the centre of the large flower brooch, was a wedding present from the late Dr John Williamson. In the year of her Coronation the Queen had it made up into the jonquil-shaped spray with curved petals of navette cut diamonds which she wears here.

by a brood of mongrel dogs who bedded down on his Persian carpets and Chippendale chairs. His fortune gave him a permanent distrust of women. He had no confidence that a woman could care for him as a man rather than a millionaire – and the Williamson mine was producing 500,000 carats a year and bringing its owner an annual personal profit of £2 million. Handling his diamonds – but only the big gem stones – seemed to give him his only real happiness.

He had a passionate personal attachment to the Royal Family. When Princess Elizabeth was to be married he made a gift to her of the world's most perfect rose-pink diamond. Weighing 54 carats in

65   The Queen wears her tiara with cabochon emeralds. To match it she wears an emerald and diamond necklace inherited from Queen Mary, with both earrings and bracelet of emeralds and diamonds.

the rough, it was exquisitely cut to 23.6 carats, but for many years the Princess was undecided how to have it set. Finally, in the year of her coronation, the Queen had the Williamson Pink set in the centre of a flower spray brooch, jonquil-shaped, with curved petals of navette-cut diamonds, the flower on a stem of baguette diamonds, with two large navette-cut diamonds, one on each side of the stalk, to represent leaves. The brooch measures $4\frac{1}{2}$ inches from tip to tip, and among the many occasions on which the Queen has worn it was the wedding of the Duke and Duchess of Kent at York Minster in 1961. By that time Dr Williamson was dead.

From the Sheikh of Bahrein came pearl and diamond drop earrings (Plate 44) which Her Majesty frequently wears on informal occasions.

44   These pearl and diamond drop ear-rings were a wedding present to the Queen from the Sheikh of Bahrein.

87   Queen Elizabeth wearing one of the bow brooches made by Garrards in 1858 for Queen Victoria.

45 & 46   The magnificent Diamond Diadem, one of the Crown Jewels, was
made for King George IV and was worn by Queen Victoria, Queen Alexandra
and Queen Mary, passing to the Queen on her Accession. Her Majesty wears it
on the annual drive to Westminster for the State Opening of Parliament.

47 & 48   Queen Alexandra and Queen Mary wearing the Diamond Diadem.

Prince Philip's personal gift to his bride was a broad bracelet of diamonds. The wedding ring was a plain narrow band of Welsh gold, far removed from the ornate style of the wedding ring King Edward VII, as Prince of Wales, gave to Princess Alexandra. This was a broad keeper set with a Beryl, an Emerald, a Ruby, a Turquoise, a Jacinth and another Emerald – the initials of the gems spelling out his name BERTIE.

On the 6th of February 1952 when King George VI died, and Princess Elizabeth ascended to the throne she became possessed of the wealth of personal jewellery vested in the Crown Jewels, which comprise, beyond the Regalia, many magnificent ornaments which have been secured to the Throne though once the personal possessions of past sovereigns. Foremost is the Diamond Diadem (Plate 45) which had been worn by Queen Victoria (Plate 46), Queen Alexandra (Plate 47), Queen Mary (Plate 48), and which Her Majesty (Plate 49) was to wear on her way to her Coronation and whilst driving each year in the Irish State Coach for the State Opening of Parliament. (For the ceremony of the Queen's Speech the Queen wears the Imperial State Crown (Plate 131).

49   Her Majesty wears the Diamond Diadem, with diamond and pearl ear-
rings and the Jubilee Necklace in this portrait by Lord Snowdon.

50   The diamond collet necklace worn here by Queen Victoria is part of the
Crown Jewellery, and is seen being worn by Her Majesty in Plate 1 and by Queen
Mary in Plate 86.

The Diamond Diadem, which is completely circular, was made for King George IV to wear outside a Cap of State on his way to his Coronation in 1821, although there is no proof that he ever wore it. George IV did not use either St Edward's Crown or the State Crown for his Coronation, deciding to have a new crown made, in which he wanted jewelled roses, thistles and shamrocks instead of fleurs-de-lis, which he considered French. The Heralds, however, declared that fleurs-de-lis had been used in England since the time of Edward the Confessor, and would not sanction the change. The Monarch therefore had his way by including the 'national' emblems in his diadem. The jewels were hired for King George IV's coronation but the diadem was subsequently reset with permanent jewels for Queen Victoria's Coronation in June 1838. The diadem has four crosses pattées, the front cross pattée containing a straw-coloured diamond in its centre, and four bouquets in diamonds of the rose, shamrock and thistle. The band is composed of diamond scroll work and the bands of pearls, remounted by order of Queen Alexandra, have 81 pearls in the upper band and 88 in the lower.

Another personal piece of Crown Jewellery which the Queen wore on her Coronation Day is the diamond collet necklace with a drop-shape diamond suspended from the centre collet (Plate 51), originally made for Queen Victoria (Plate 50) matched by a pair of large diamond collet top and drop-shape diamond ear-rings. The necklace was originally made for Victoria from 28 brilliant collets taken from a Garter Badge and from a Ceremonial Sword, of which the nine largest stones weigh between $11\frac{1}{4}$ and $8\frac{1}{4}$ carats. The large drop-shape diamond from the Timur Ruby Necklace was later set in this piece, and this stone was in 1937 slightly trimmed, as has been recounted, to be put in the Crown of Queen Elizabeth, now the Queen Mother, for her Coronation, which Princess Elizabeth attended. The diamond drop has since been put back on the necklace, which, with the ear-rings, Queen Elizabeth II often now wears for evening functions. Both Queen Mary (Plate 86) and Queen Elizabeth The Queen Mother (Plate 2) have worn this necklace.

A very attractive Victorian necklace, which the Queen wore at her first State Opening of Parliament in November 1952, is the Jubilee Necklace (Plates 52 & 53) which was presented to Queen Victoria by

51   A detailed study of the diamond collet necklace with a drop-shaped diamond suspended from the centre collet, originally made from the gems from a Garter Badge and sword, and now supplemented by diamond drop ear-rings.

the Daughters of the Empire to celebrate her Jubilee in 1887. It consists of graduated trefoils of diamonds each with a pearl centre. The centrepiece of the necklace is a quatrefoil of diamonds surrounding a pearl. Hanging from this is a large pearl pendant and, resting on the quatrefoil, a pearl and diamond crown.

52 & 53   The fine Jubilee Necklace, of graduated trefoils of diamonds each
with a pearl centre, the centre-piece of the necklace being a quatrefoil of diamonds
surrounding a pearl, with a pearl pendant and diamond crown. Originally made
for Queen Victoria's Jubilee in 1887, it is worn by Queen Elizabeth with pearl
and diamond drop ear-rings.

54, 55, 56 & 57   A large sapphire brooch with twelve diamonds, given by Prince Albert to Queen Victoria on their marriage in 1840, was worn, right, by Queen Alexandra on her Coronation Day and, in much simpler fashion by Her Majesty today. Queen Elizabeth the Queen Mother also wore the brooch during the lifetime of King George VI.

A double string of pearls, with a diamond clasp belonged to
Queen Mary. The Queen inherited them from her grandmother
(Plate 27). She wears them for daytime and at informal evening
occasions.

Two historical brooches came to the Queen on her accession. One,
a large sapphire surrounded by twelve diamonds (Plate 54), was given
by Prince Albert to Queen Victoria for their marriage in 1840.
Queen Alexandra wore it for her Coronation in 1902 – (Plate 55)
shows just how much jewellery Queen Alexandra did wear on her
Coronation Day – it is worn simply by the Queen today (Plate 56).
The brooch was often worn by Queen Elizabeth the Queen Mother
(Plate 57) during the lifetime of King George VI, as was another
Crown Jewel, a brooch consisting of a large diamond surrounded by
smaller ones, which the Queen is wearing in the photograph (Plate

58   A diamond brooch consisting of a large gem surrounded by smaller ones, a Crown Jewel which the Queen often wears. The Queen Mother is seen wearing it in Plate 2.

59   The large pearl drop ear-rings with a diamond stud are a part of the Crown Jewels which came to the Queen on her Accession.

58). The Queen Mother wore this brooch at the neck of her Coronation dress in 1937, and the picture of her in her Coronation robes (Plate 2) makes an interesting contrast with Queen Alexandra. Another set of jewellery which came to the Queen as Sovereign was the pair of large pearl drop ear-rings with a diamond stud, which she is often seen wearing at evening functions (Plate 59).

The Coronation of Her Majesty Queen Elizabeth II was an occasion for many gifts being made to her, but undoubtedly the most outstanding new jewellery which she accepted was a necklace

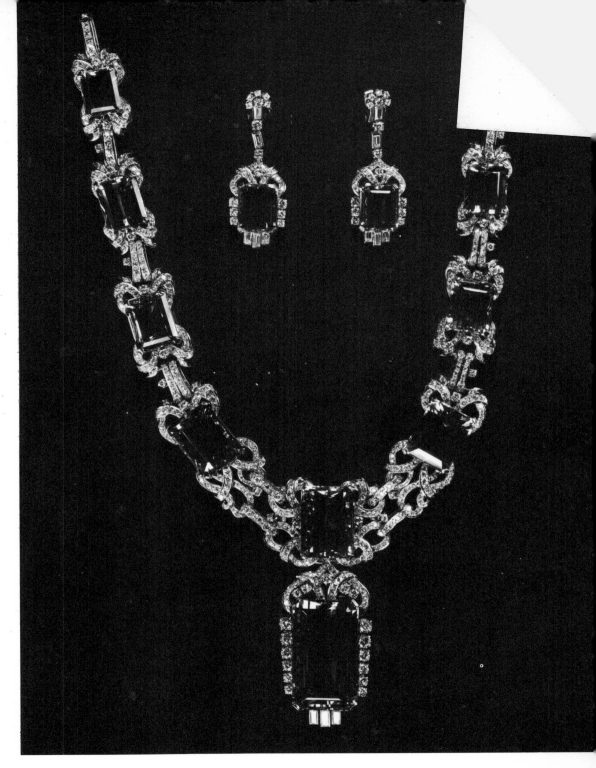

60   A necklace and matching ear-rings of large square-cut aquamarines and diamonds, stones which took a year to collect, were the Queen's Coronation present from the President and People of Brazil.

61   The Queen was so delighted with the gift from Brazil that she had a small tiara of aquamarines and diamonds made to go with it. The Brazilians responded with a further gift of a bracelet of seven giant aquamarines set in clusters of diamond crowns. The Queen, wearing the complete suite in the picture, has removed the pendant of the necklace.

62   This fringed necklace of drop diamonds set with brilliants and baguettes was presented to the Queen by King Faisal of Saudi Arabia during his State visit to Britain in 1967.

and matching ear-rings of large square-cut aquamarines and diamonds (Plate 60) given by the President and People of Brazil. The gift of these nine graduated large oblong aquamarines in a scroll setting with the fine aquamarine oblong drop, and the matching stones for the ear-rings, had taken the Brazilians a whole year to collect, for stocks of the gems were low and a fine match was deemed necessary. But the Queen was so delighted with it that she had made a small tiara of aquamarines and diamonds which she wore with it (Plate 61). Then the Brazilians collected fresh stones, and in 1958 supplemented their Coronation Gift with a bracelet of seven great aquamarines set in hundreds of diamonds clustered into small crowns. It will be seen that the Queen, who wears the tiara,

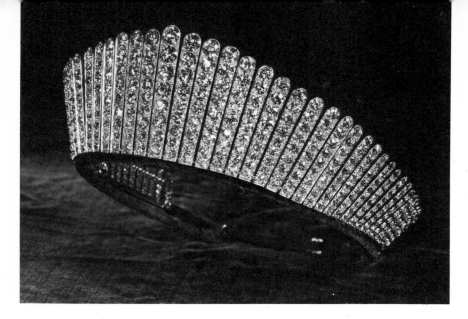

63 The Russian-style fringed diamond tiara which had been Queen Alexandra's silver wedding present was bequeathed by Queen Mary to Her Majesty. Queen Alexandra can be seen wearing it in Plate 8 and Her Majesty in Plate 7. Queen Mary is wearing it in Plate 9.

64 The Queen's most distinctive tiara. In the centre of each of the fifteen interlaced circles of diamonds hangs a cabochon emerald, but these can be interchanged for fifteen drop pearls.

66　Queen Mary wearing the emerald and diamond necklace, part of a suite the emeralds of which came from the daughter-in-law of King George III, Augusta, Duchess of Cambridge, Queen Mary's grandmother.

necklace and bracelet and ear-rings in one suite, has since 1957 shortened the necklace by removing the pendant.

During the State Visit to Britain in May 1967 of King Faisal of Saudi Arabia a modern diamond necklace was given to the Queen. It is a fringe of drop diamonds set with brilliants and baguettes (Plate 62).

Little more than a year after the accession of Queen Elizabeth II, on the 24th of March 1953, her beloved grandmother Queen Mary died, and bequeathed to her the remaining principal pieces of jewellery.

There were three tiaras. One was the Russian style diamond fringe tiara (Plate 63) which had been given to Queen Alexandra by friends in 1888 as a silver wedding present. The sunray style was developed in the Russian Court where the fashion was to wear

67　The emerald and diamond necklace, with two drops of uneven length consisting of a large emerald and the sixth part of the Cullinan diamond set as a marquise pendant.

STUDY BY DONALD MCKAGUE

68   Queen Mary wears the interchangeable tiara with drop pearls instead of emeralds.

69   Her Majesty wears the tiara with drop pearls within the diamond circles, and with the Jubilee Necklace of pearls and diamonds.

jewelled tiaras shaped like the head-dresses of girl peasants. Queen Mary, had often worn it (Plate 9) and Queen Elizabeth has worn it for many State occasions (Plate 27) including the Opening of Parliament in Australia, New Zealand, Canada and Malta.

The next tiara is perhaps the most fascinating in the Queen's collection of eight. It is of fifteen interlaced circles of diamonds in the centre of each of which can be hung either fifteen cabochon emeralds (as in the still life picture, Plate 64) or fifteen drop pearls. In the colour picture (Plate 65) the Queen is wearing the tiara with emeralds, and with it she is wearing an emerald and diamond necklace, also inherited from Queen Mary, (Plate 66) with ear-rings and one emerald and diamond bracelet. The complete emerald suite consists of the drops for the tiara, the necklace, ear-rings, two bracelets, a brooch and a stomacher. The emeralds in the tiara and the matching necklace originally belonged to Augusta, Duchess of Cambridge, daughter-in-law of King George III and mother of the Duchess of Teck, who gave them to Princess Mary, Duchess of

70, 71 & 72 Queen Mary's former tiara, bequeathed to Her Majesty: a diamond tiara with nineteen pearl drops hanging below a lover's knot in diamonds. The tiara can be seen worn by Queen Mary and Queen Elizabeth.

73   The Dagmar Necklace, in pearls and diamonds, given to Princess
Alexandra by her father, King Frederick VII of Denmark.

Teck, the mother of Queen Mary. The two drops on the necklace
(seen in detail, Plate 67), which hang at uneven lengths are a large
emerald and a marquise pendant diamond of $11\frac{3}{4}$ carats which is the
sixth part of the Cullinan Diamond. (The Cullinan is discussed in
detail on Page 72). When the Queen wears this 'convertible' tiara
with the fifteen drop pearls – which was the original conception:
it was Queen Mary's idea to have the emerald interchange – she
often wears it with the Jubilee Necklace in pearls and diamonds
(Plate 69). The third tiara bequeathed by Queen Mary is of diamonds
with 19 hanging pearl drops and a lover's knot in diamonds above
each pearl (Plate 70).

74 & 75   Queen Alexandra wore the Dagmar Necklace as a stomacher for her Coronation, and Queen Elizabeth *(facing page)* has had the pendant cross and two pearl drops removed.

The Queen inherited from her grandmother two necklaces: the emerald and diamond necklace which has just been described, and the Dagmar Necklace, an elaborately looped necklace in pearls and diamonds (Plate 73). It was given to Princess Alexandra by her father, King Frederick VII of Denmark, on the occasion of his daughter's marriage to the Prince of Wales, afterwards King Edward VII. Princess Alexandra had an ill-fated sister, Princess Dagmar, who was betrothed to the Russian Tsarevitch but died before the marriage: but the necklace, though it may have had more poignant associations to Queen Alexandra because of this tragedy, was not named after her sister but after an ancient Queen of Denmark in whose grave was found a gold and enamel eleventh-century cross; a replica of this cross formed a pendant to the necklace. Queen Alexandra wore the jewellery (Plate 74) on her Coronation Day, but not around her neck. It was worn to decorate the top of her dress among many rows of pearls. The Queen now wears it (Plate 75) without the pendant cross and without two pearl drops which hung on either side of the centre of the necklace. She wore this piece at a Gala Ballet in Copenhagen during her State Visit to Denmark and in London when the King of Denmark invited her and the Duke of Edinburgh to a banquet at the Dorchester Hotel.

76 & 77   The choker pearl necklace with diamond and sapphire front clasp, perhaps the most characteristic of Queen Mary's personal jewellery, is worn with completely different effect by Queen Elizabeth, who inherited it from her grandmother.

The Queen has worn most effectively (Plate 76) another inheritance which is perhaps one of the most characteristic pieces of Queen Mary's jewellery (Plate 77), the choker pearl necklace with a diamond and sapphire clasp in the front.

The sobriquet "Granny's Chips" which the Queen often uses, masks the pieces which make up the Queen's most valuable brooch, also inherited from Queen Mary (Plate 78): a pear-shaped diamond of 92 carats and a square diamond of 62 carats which are the third and fourth parts of the Cullinan Diamond (Plate 79).

The Cullinan was the largest gem diamond crystal ever discovered in the world. In the rough it weighed 3,025 carats, about one pound and a half. It was found at the Premier Mine, 300 miles north-east of Kimberley, in 1905. The mine superintendent, Frederick Wells, was making an inspection trip when his attention was caught by a stone embedded in the side of the pit reflecting the rays of the setting sun. He thought he might be the victim of a joke, working on a piece of glass especially 'salted' there for him to find. But the stone proved to

78, 79 & 80   The most valuable brooch in the world is that made from the third and fourth parts of the Cullinan Diamond. It consists of a square-cut gem of 62 carats from which hangs a pear-shaped diamond of 92 carats. Queen Mary, to whom it came as a personal possession, wore it across her Garter ribbon. Queen Elizabeth wears it as a lapel brooch in this record of her visit to the Amsterdam workshop of Asscher's, the firm which originally cut the Cullinan Diamond in 1907.

ASSCHER'S DIAMANT MAATSCHAPPIJ N.V.

be a genuine diamond with three natural faces and a cleavage face that suggested that it had once been even larger.

The stone was called the Cullinan, after Sir Thomas Cullinan, chairman of the Premier Diamond Company. The rough diamond was bought by the Transvaal Government in 1907 for presentation to King Edward VII on his 66th birthday in November of that year. It was a magnificent gesture by Prime Minister Botha indicating final reconciliation after the South African War, but the King learned that the voting for the presentation in the South African Parliament had been 42-19, and he hesitated to accept a gift from one of his Dominions when there had not been unanimous agreement amongst the donors. But equally he could not give mortal offence to the Boers who had made the gesture – ironically it was the English settlers who had voted against the presentation. Accordingly, at his birthday Drawing Room at Sandringham, he accepted the great cloudy stone but turned to Queen Alexandra and gave it to her. He asked the envoys to tell the people of the Transvaal that it would be set in the Queen's Crown.

But when the stone was examined by Asschers in Amsterdam it was clear that, because of one fault, more than one gem must be made out of it. On the 10th of February 1908 Mr J. Asscher was ready to cleave the Cullinan. He placed the cleaving blade on the stone and tapped it with a heavy rod. The steel blade broke – but not the Cullinan. On the second attempt the stone came apart exactly as planned. And the one who collapsed this time was Mr Asscher. Overcome with the tension, he fainted.

The two pieces of the Cullinan were cleaved again, and the pieces resulting were further subdivided until the total yield of the Cullinan was nine major gems, 96 small brilliants, and more than nine carats of polished fragments.

The largest gem from the Cullinan is known as the Great Star of Africa, a pear-shaped diamond with 74 facets and weighing $516\frac{1}{2}$ carats, the largest cut diamond in the world. King Edward ordered it to be placed in the State Sceptre With The Cross, where it is on permanent display in the new underground Crown Jewel House at Waterloo Barracks within the Tower of London. The second

81   In this portrait Queen Mary is wearing the Cullinan V diamond on the emerald and diamond stomacher, also Cullinan VIII, and a diamond scroll brooch with cabochon emerald centre with the cabochon emerald drop hanging from the Cullinan VIII. Also a cabochon emerald brooch surrounded by two circles of diamonds with a cabochon emerald drop. All these pieces have now been inherited by Queen Elizabeth.

82   Here Queen Mary wears Cullinan III and Cullinan IV as a pendant to her necklace, and she is also wearing Cullinan V, Cullinan VII and Cullinan VIII.

gem, known as Cullinan II, is still the second largest cut diamond in the world, weighing $309\frac{1}{4}$ carats, and is set in the brow of the Imperial State Crown. They are however removable and have been worn by Queen Mary as a brooch.

The Star of Africa and Cullinan II are Crown Jewels. The rest of the Cullinan gems are private property, because it had been a part of the cleaving contract with Asschers that the remaining gems were to be considered the 'clippings' and given to the cutter as the fee for his work. King Edward immediately bought a third stone, now Cullinan VI, a marquise diamond of $11\frac{3}{4}$ carats, and made a present of it to Queen Alexandra. All the remainder, the six major gems, 96 brilliants and nine carats of fragments, were bought by the South African Government and eventually presented to Queen Mary, thus becoming her personal property, to bequeath at will, in contrast to the State classification of the two largest gems.

Cullinan III and IV, the diamonds of 92 and 62 carats respectively, form the brooch which Queen Elizabeth II inherited, and the term 'Granny's Chips' seems a remarkably playful description. The diamonds had been placed in the new crown made for Queen Mary on the occasion of King George V's Coronation 1911. The third part being placed in the surmounting cross, the fourth set in the circlet of the crown.

When the Queen visited the Netherlands in March 1958 she wore the brooch during a tour of the Asscher Factory see (Plate 80) this was the first time the diamonds had been back to Holland in 50 years.

Cullinan V: a heart shaped diamond of $18\frac{3}{8}$ carats was set with other diamonds in a brooch worn by Queen Mary as the centre of the first cross pattée of the circlet of her crown at the coronation of George VI in place of the Koh-i-noor which was mounted in the Crown of Queen Elizabeth the Consort. It is now a favourite brooch of the Queen's (Plate 121). It belongs to the emerald and diamond Suite as worn by Queen Mary (Plate 81).

Cullinan VI: the Marquise diamond given by King Edward to Queen Alexandra is the drop pendant in the emerald and diamond necklace (Plate 67).

83   Her Majesty wears as a brooch the diamond Cullinan VII, a marquise of over 9 carats, with Cullinan VIII, a brilliant of unusual oblong shape.

Cullinan VII: a Marquise of $9\frac{3}{16}$ carats is a pendant on a diamond brooch (Plate 83) owned by the Queen, the centre of the brooch is Cullinan VIII, a $6\frac{3}{8}$ brilliant carat of unusual oblong shape. (Plate 81) shows Queen Mary wearing the 8th part of the Cullinan. (Plate 82) shows her wearing the 7th and 8th part.

Cullinan IX: a pear shaped diamond of $4\frac{9}{32}$ carats was mounted by Queen Mary in a ring with a claw setting which she bequeathed to Queen Elizabeth but which Her Majesty rarely wears.

A cabochon emerald brooch surrounded by two circles of diamonds with a large cabochon emerald drop (Plate 84) and a diamond scroll brooch with a cabochon emerald centre and a cabochon emerald drop (Plate 85) were also inherited from her grandmother (Plate 81).

84 A cabochon emerald brooch surrounded by two circles of diamonds with a large cabochon emerald drop was inherited by Queen Elizabeth from her grandmother.

85 This diamond scroll brooch with a cabochon emerald centre and a cabochon emerald drop was also inherited from Queen Mary by Queen Elizabeth. Also see Plate 67.

86 Among the jewels which Queen Mary wore for her Coronation were three diamond brooches made by Garrards in 1858 from Queen Victoria's diamonds. See also Plates 88 and 89.

91 (*right*) With pearl drops in her interchangeable tiara worn with the Jubilee Necklace, Queen Elizabeth also wears a large diamond bow brooch with a pearl drop, inherited from Queen Mary.

97 A cabochon sapphire brooch surrounded by two circles of diamonds with a pearl drop. Queen Mary is shown wearing this brooch in Plate 96.

114 In 1954 the Commonwealth of Australia presented to the Queen the spray of wattle with three ti-tree blossoms, with rare yellow diamonds representing the wattle (the emblem of Australia) and blue-white diamond baguettes used for the leaves.

88 & 89 Queen Elizabeth the Queen Mother wearing one of the diamond bow brooches (see Plate 86) soon after the Accession of King George VI. Two of the brooches are shown in detail.

A favourite bow brooch of Her Majesty (Plate 88) belongs to a set of three diamond bow brooches two large and one small, these were mounted by Garrards in May 1858 with diamonds supplied by Queen Victoria. Queen Alexandra and Queen Mary both wore them on their coronation dresses (Photos 74 and 86) and two were owned by Queen Elizabeth the Queen Mother. Plate 89 shows her wearing one. Amongst the other jewels which the Queen inherited from her Grandmother are:– A true lovers knot in diamonds (Plate 90) which Her Majesty wore at Princess Margaret's wedding in

90   The true lover's knot in diamonds was pinned to the ribbon of the Order
worn by Queen Elizabeth on her State visit to Brussels. It had been bequeathed
by Queen Mary.

1960, and a large diamond bow brooch with a pearl drop (Plate 91),
a wedding gift to Queen Mary (Plate 92) from Kensington where
she spent her childhood. Queen Mary wore this brooch at her
coronation in 1911.

92   A large diamond bow brooch with a pearl drop, seen as it was worn at the
Coronation of King Edward VII by Queen Mary, who also wore it at her own
Coronation.

93   A family treasure originally belonging to Queen Mary's mother is the pearl brooch surrounded by three circles of diamonds, one circle being of double plaited diamonds; a hanging half-circle containing six diamonds and a large diamond fall from the main brooch and three pearl drops hang from the half-circle.

94 & 95   The diamond brooch with two diamond drops and a pearl drop *(top right)* was originally a wedding present to Queen Mary. Queen Mary wore this diamond brooch at the christening of Princess Anne.

96   A cabochon sapphire brooch surrounded by two circles of diamonds with
a pearl drop, worn here by Queen Mary, was originally a wedding present made
by King Edward VII and Queen Alexandra to Queen Alexandra's sister, the
Empress Marie Feodorovna of Russia.

98 The cabochon sapphire and diamond brooch which the Queen is wearing
here was a wedding present to Queen Mary.

A Pearl brooch surrounded by three circles of diamonds, one
circle being of double plaited diamonds. A hanging half-circle
containing six diamonds and one large diamond fall from the main
brooch and three pearl drops hang from the half-circle (Plate 93).
Queen Mary inherited this from her mother, the Duchess of Teck,
and Queen Elizabeth wore it at Princess Alexandra's wedding in
1963. There is also a diamond brooch with two diamond drops and
one pearl drop (Plate 94) which was a wedding present to Queen
Mary from the Women of Hampshire and which she wore at the
christening of her great granddaughter, Princess Anne (Plate 95);
and a cabochon sapphire brooch surrounded by two circles of
diamonds with a pearl drop (Plate 96) which was originally a
wedding present from King Edward VII and Queen Alexandra to
Queen Alexandra's sister, the Empress Marie Feodorovna who married Alexander III of Russia. The Empress gave to Queen Mary as a
wedding present a cabochon sapphire and diamond brooch (Plate
98) which the Queen now has – it is noticed that Her Majesty sometimes wears this brooch upside down.

99 & 100   Ear-rings which formerly belonged to Queen Mary: *(left)* drop pearl ear-rings with the pearl suspended inside a frame of diamonds; *(right)* one diamond surrounded by seven others.

The Queen now possesses six pairs of ear-rings which formerly belonged to her grandmother. The drop pearl ear-rings with the pearl suspended inside a frame of diamonds (Plate 99) are often worn when Her Majesty wears the pearls in her 'convertible' tiara of interlaced circles of diamonds. With the diamond fringe tiara or the diamond tiara of festoons, scrolls and collet spikes she often wears

101 & 102   Queen Mary wearing the ear-rings seen in Plates 100 and 103.

the ear-rings consisting of one diamond surrounded by seven others
(Plate 100). The ear rings consisting of a large pearl surrounded by
ten diamonds (Plate 103) were also worn by Queen Alexandra and
Queen Mary (Plates 74 , 102). They match Her Majesty's diamond
and pearl Jubilee necklace. The ear-rings with a small diamond stud
and a large pearl (Plate 104) were worn by Queen Mary at the
christening both of Prince Charles and Princess Anne (Plate 95, and
Queen Elizabeth, who often wears them for evening functions wore
them also at the weddings of Princess Margaret and Princess
Alexandra.

103   The Queen wearing ear-rings consisting of a large pearl surrounded by ten diamonds.

104 & 105   Ear-rings with a small diamond stud and a large pearl.

Two other diamond stud ear-rings (Plates 106 & 107) were also bequeathed by Queen Mary to Her Majesty.

The grand evening wear bracelets which passed from Queen Mary include the broad bracelet of diamond links and chains (Plates 102 & 108), which she frequently wears; a bracelet of four rows of pearls with a sapphire clasp surrounded by diamonds, which was once worn by Queen Alexandra and belongs to a set of two, but the Queen usually wears only one (Plate 109); and bracelets of five rows of pearls with a diamond clasp (Plates 110 & 111) and diamonds with square-cut emeralds (Plates 112 and 113).

106 & 107   Two other diamond stud ear-rings left to Queen Elizabeth by her grandmother.

Queen Mary's bequests, coming as they did in one transference, clearly constitute the most notable large addition to the Queen's private treasures of mounted jewellery, though her inheritance from her father, King George VI, of the separate gems in the possession of the Royal Family must not be ignored. In addition, on various occasions the Queen is the recipient of gifts from kinsfolk, friends, corporations and countries who wish to mark, or create, an 'occasion'. A rare ornament is the brooch holding a spray of 150 diamonds which was presented by the Commonwealth of Australia to the Queen during her State Visit to Canberra in 1954 (Plate 114a). The

108 & 109   Bracelets worn by Queen Elizabeth which were inherited from Queen Mary include, *(left)* a broad bracelet of diamond links and chains, here worn by Queen Mary and seen worn by Queen Elizabeth in Plate 103; *(right)* a bracelet of four rows of pearls with a sapphire clasp surrounded by diamonds.

brooch is in the form of a spray of wattle with three ti-tree blossoms in the centre. (The wattle is the emblem of Australia, and ti-trees are a Polynesian species with edible roots). To represent the wattle, buyers searched the diamond centres of the world for the rare

110 & 111   Five rows of pearls with a diamond clasp, worn here by Queen
Mary and by Queen Elizabeth.

112 & 113   A wide bracelet of diamonds with square-cut emeralds. The Queen
is seen wearing it in Plate 113.

yellow diamonds (so-called: in fact they are white stones traced with yellow, and are regarded as collectors' pieces rather than fashionable stones). The wattle leaves are blue-white diamond baguettes, and the diamonds representing the ti-tree blossoms are centred with a blue-white diamond, each of five carats. The brooch, which measures four inches from tip to tip, was designed and made

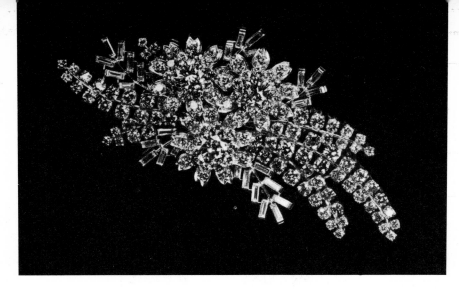

114a   A close-up of the wattle brooch in colour plate 114.

in Australia, and the Queen wore it the very next day after she had received it, when she took the salute at a parade of ex-servicemen by the George V Memorial in front of the Parliament House at Canberra. She wore the spray when she returned to Australia in 1963 (Plate 114). Previously in 1963 she visited New Zealand, and wore the diamond fern brooch, representing the emblem of that Dominion, which she had been given on Christmas Day, 1953, by the Women of Auckland (Plate 115).

115   This diamond fern brooch—the New Zealand emblem—was given to the Queen by the Women of Auckland on Christmas Day 1953.

116 The jewelled brooch representing a multi-coloured basket of flowers was given to the Queen by her parents.

117 The Queen was given this flower brooch in pink and blue sapphires before she came to the Throne.

A present from the Queen's parents is the brooch of a multi-coloured basket of flowers (Plate 116), which the Queen wore for the first photographs taken of herself with her son, Prince Charles, when he was scarcely a month old. The small flower brooch in pink and blue sapphires (Plate 117) was a present made to the Queen while she

118   The Queen wears a diamond watch with a wide diamond strap.

was still Princess Elizabeth. Another gift, a diamond watch with
an oblong face and wide diamond strap, is worn constantly by the
Queen at evening functions (Plate 118). The Swiss Federal Republic
presented as a wedding gift the diamond watch with a strap of single
diamonds with, joining the strap to the circular face, a ring of diamonds (Plate 119). But the watch to which the Queen most clearly
lost her heart was given to her when she was twelve years old. It was
a platinum watch reputed to be the smallest in the world, and it was
given to the Queen, now the Queen Mother, on Princess Elizabeth's
behalf when King George VI and Queen Elizabeth made a State
Visit to France in 1938. President Lebrun presented it on behalf of

PORTRAIT STUDY BY DONALD MCKAGUE OF TORONTO
119   This diamond watch with a strap of single diamonds was presented to the
Queen by the Swiss Federal Republic on the occasion of her marriage.

120   The smallest watch in the world, a replica of the Queen's favourite watch, which she wore since she was twelve. The original was lost at Sandringham, and the French presented her with a copy during her State visit to Paris.

121 The day watch with a wide gold strap, worn here by the Queen, was a gift from Canada when she toured the Dominion in 1951. Her Majesty is also wearing a favourite heart-shaped brooch containing the fifth part of the Cullinan Diamond.

France. The Princess wore it daily for seventeen years until, after her accession, she lost it at Sandringham and the most careful searches could not unearth it. In April 1957 she herself paid a State Visit to France and French statesmen, having heard of her loss, presented her with a replica (Plate 120), which she wore next day at a reception she held in the British Embassy. Her day watch with a wide gold strap was given to her in Canada when she toured the Dominion in 1951 (Plate 121).

123   A triple diamond collet necklace made from unmounted gems in the Royal collection.

125   The Queen had this triple row of graduated pearls made up from family jewels.

Clearly the Queen, knowing what she likes, occasionally decides to create some piece of jewellery. The Williamson Pink brooch was the culmination of her own ideas on the use of this unique diamond. Recently she has worn a sapphire and diamond tiara (Plate 122) which she has added to her private collection, and which matches her sapphire and diamond necklace (Plate 14), the nineteenth century piece with its matching ear-rings which her parents gave her as a wedding present. Before King George VI died, he took 105 unmounted diamond collets from the family jewels and had them made into the triple diamond collet necklace (Plate 123), with a single row at the back joined on each side with a diamond triangular motif – a piece which the Queen has worn a number of times for the State Opening of Parliament and on many evening functions. Another private piece of the Queen's jewellery is the necklace of round rubies set in diamonds with three ruby drops also set in diamonds (Plate 124): this was first worn during Her Majesty's State Visit to Germany in 1965.

Soon after her accession the Queen had a triple row of graduated pearls made up from the family jewels, and, after a couple of years had the top row extended (Plate 125), since when this pearl necklace has been a great favourite for daytime wear. She decided on a modern design for a diamond and ruby brooch (Plate 126). Another personal brooch (Plate 127) has a frosted gold sunflower with a diamond centre and a diamond on each petal. The pearl stud ear-rings shown in (Plate 128) were worn for the first time only a month after she had her ears pierced in August 1951. She varies them with the ear-rings (Plate 129) consisting of a small diamond stud and a small pearl which she likes for daytime functions. For evening wear, one of her most striking private pieces is the bracelet of diamond circles (Plate 130) which has in the centre of each circle a black and a natural pearl set alternately.

122   The Queen wears a new sapphire and diamond tiara
to match her sapphire and diamond necklace (Plate 14)
given to her by the King on her wedding day.

124   During her visit to Malta in November 1967, the Queen is seen
wearing a necklace of round rubies set in diamonds with three ruby
drops also set in diamonds.

131 *Above left* The Imperial Crown of State, set with 3,250 diamonds and precious stones, including Saint Edward's sapphire, the Black Prince's ruby, and the second Cullinan diamond.

132 *Above right* Saint Edward's Crown.

133 *Left* The head of the Sceptre with the Cross, bearing the largest diamond in the world, the Great Star of Africa.

126   With her triple row of pearls the Queen wears a diamond and ruby brooch of modern design.

127 & 128   A frosted gold sunflower with a diamond centre and a diamond on each petal makes this unusual Royal brooch. The Queen's ear-rings include the simple pearl studs, right.

129   Ear-rings of diamond studs with pearl below.

130 The bracelet of diamond circles with a black and a natural pearl set alternately in each circle is one of the Queen's most striking pieces of jewellery.

The Regalia

Many of the most striking of the Crown Jewels have been described in connection with their use at formal State occasions by Her Majesty. There are certain pieces of Regalia which are considered either too sacred (as Saint Edward's Crown) to be worn outside the Sanctuary, or which are for practical reasons rarely touched at occasions other than a Coronation or a Sovereign's Funeral.

Saint Edward's Crown (Plate 132) is not a direct link with King Edward the Confessor, since almost every trace of the English Regalia was destroyed under Oliver Cromwell's régime (though even Cromwell affected a crown before he died). The present Crown of that name is the one made in 1662 for King Charles II. Formerly it was set with paste and imitation pearls until the time of a Coronation, when it was mounted with real gems. Today it is permanently set with diamonds and precious and semi-precious stones: sapphire, cape ruby, amethyst, tourmaline, white topaz, yellow topaz, spinel, peridot, carbuncle, garnet, jargoon and rose diamond, with silver pearls.

The Imperial Crown of State (Plate 131) is assumed by the Sovereign shortly after the actual crowning, since the weight of Saint Edward's Crown is too heavy to wear for a long time. On a gold frame are set 3,250 diamonds and precious stones, which include Saint Edward's sapphire, the Black Prince's Ruby, Queen Elizabeth's ear-rings, the Stuart sapphire, and Cullinan II. The Monarch wears this Crown at the ceremonial Opening of Parliament, but proceeds to Westminster wearing the Diamond Diadem (Plate 46).

The Sceptre With The Cross (Plate 133) is a gold rod $36\frac{1}{4}$ inches long weighing 2 lbs. 12 oz. and set with 272 diamonds, 25 rubies, 12 emeralds, a sapphire, an amethyst and – making it the most valuable sceptre in the world – the great Star of Africa at its head, the largest brilliant in existence.

The Orb, of jewelled gold, weighs over 42 ounces, and is encrusted with rubies, emeralds, sapphires and diamonds, bordered by rows of pearls of which there are over 400.

Glossary

AMETHYST: a species of quartz, of a violet, purple or blue shade. The name of the stone has a curious origin, coming from a Greek word meaning 'not drunken', because the gem was supposed to have the power of preventing the wearer from becoming intoxicated. Although tinged quartz is found in many places throughout the world, pure Amethyst is rarely found outside India and Ceylon – with the exception of Scotland, which explains why Amethyst is one of the principal stones set in old Scottish jewellery.

BAGUETTE: a straight-sided stone cut in the form of narrow rectangles, used to form patterns in jewellery; a baguette cut is often used for the sidestone in a ring.

BERYL: a mineral crystal which when transparent is known as Precious Beryl, while opaque varieties are called Common Beryl. The transparent green variety is the Emerald (but a less brilliant precious stone would still be called a Beryl). An Aquamarine is chemically a bluish-green Precious Beryl.

side view

BRILLIANT: a diamond cut according to the method introduced by the Venetian Vincenti Peruzzi in the late seventeenth century, which 'traps' most light within the stone by intricate refraction. The modern version of the brilliant cut has 33 facets on the top half and 25 on the bottom. Since a brilliant is circular it is a favourite cut for stones for engagement rings. In tiny sizes brilliants are used as sidestones on rings.

CABOCHON: possibly the oldest method of shaping gemstones. The top of the stone is rounded; the base can be flat, concave or convex. The cabochon is not facetted.

CARAT: a measure used for weighing gemstones, now equal to one fifth of a gramme; there are 142 carats to the ounce. (Smaller stones are measured in points; there are 100 points to the carat.) The term Carat is also used as the qualitative measure of the purity of gold, pure gold being considered as 24 carats.

CARBUNCLE: A cabochon cut Garnet, dark red in colour.

CLAW SETTING: a method of mounting gemstones where they are held in miniature 'claws' projecting from the base of the setting.

COLLET: a method of setting in which the gem is held in place by enclosing it in a band of metal.

EMERALD CUT (also known as step cut): an oblong or square cut with the facets polished diagonally across the corners, so called because emeralds are often cut this way.

FACET: a small flat surface on a cut gemstone.

GARNET: a gemstone, usually red, but which can occur in almost any colour except blue.

JACYNTH: a variety of Zircon, of a transparent red-orange hue.

JARGOON: a translucent, colourless Zircon.

MARQUISE (or NAVETTE): a cut which leaves the stone long and narrow, pointed like a boat.

PEAR SHAPED: a cut in the shape of a pear (or a teardrop) which is often used in pendants. The world's largest diamond, at the head of the Queen's Sceptre, is pear-shaped.

PERIDOT: a bottle-green stone.

ROSE CUT: the first successful cut for diamonds, first found in seventeenth-century work. Saint Edward's Sapphire, in the Imperial State Crown, was rose-cut perhaps a century earlier. A modern rose-cut stone has a flat base and usually 24 triangular facets at the top.

SPINEL: as with Beryl, a general term for a stone of which the most precious form is the Ruby. The inferior, generally rose-coloured, stones are now called Spinels.

STOMACHER: an elaborate ornamental covering for the bosom of a dress, which can reach to the waistline.

SUITE: a matching set of jewellery, sometimes called a parure.

TOURMALINE: a stone which comes in many colours, but has a hazy look compared with clear gems.

ZIRCON: a favourite jewel of the ancient Greeks which comes in a variety of colours.

Index

JEWELLERY

PEOPLE AND ORGANIZATIONS